Arc de Triomphe de l'Étoile

Dominique Fernandes *art historian*
Gilles Plum *researcher in art history*
Isabelle Rouge *École nationale des chartes graduate*

This most monumental of all triumphal arches was constructed between 1806 and 1836. Although its original plans underwent a certain number of modifications reflecting political changes and power struggles, the Arch still retains the essence of its original concept as a powerful, unified ensemble.

Its entire decorative cycle belongs to the high tradition of sculpture of the first half of the nineteenth century. Groups, figures, friezes, and bas-reliefs are signature works by Jean-Pierre Cortot, Antoine Etex, and James Pradier. But, incontestably, the most celebrated sculpture is that by François Rude: *La Marseillaise*. With its Tomb of the Unknown Soldier and Memorial Flame, the Arch has become a revered patriotic site. The structure also represents universally a symbolic image of Paris itself.

Pl. VI.

Echelle de   5   10   15. Toises

Profil de l'Edifice sur la longueur.

Longitudinal section for a fountain in the shape of an elephant surmounted by Louis XV's statue, by engineer Ribart de Chamoust, proposed for the Place de l'Étoile (1758); gouache engraving (Paris, Musée Carnavalet).

From the Butte de Chaillot to the Place de l'Étoile

The site had been prepared patiently for over one century: in 1667, on orders from Jean-Baptiste Colbert and based on drawings by André Le Nôtre (1613-1700), respectively administrator and landscape gardener to Louis XIV, the Avenue des Champs-Élysées was opened as a western extension to the axis along the central alley of the Tuileries Gardens. The scheme then involved drawing out this perspective (visible from the central pavilion of the Tuileries Palace) to the horizon and, consequently, glorifying the Parisian residence of the King. Around 1760, Ange-Jacques Gabriel (1698-1782), First Architect to Louis XV, prolonged the axis to Courbevoie. It was he who conceived the future Place de la Concorde, while engineer Jean-Rodolphe Perronet leveled the

Chaillot hillock (between 1768 and 1774) to establish a graded, circular space (at the extreme west end of the axis), known as the Place de l'Étoile. Already by 1758, engineer Étienne Ribart de Chamoust had proposed to erect there a gigantic elephant surmounted by Louis XV's statue. Gabriel and Perronet had themselves envisaged a grand, white marble obelisk. In 1787, under Louis XVI, architect Claude-Nicolas Ledoux (1736-1806) designed a pair of tollgate pavilions at the entry to the Avenue des Champs-Élysées along the Tax Farmers' wall. At long last, in 1798, a competition was launched to terminate this perspective. Chalgrin and Fontaine made up part of the jury; however, no further action was taken to complete this project.

History

From the Bastille to the Place de l'Étoile

Chalgrin's proposal for a triumphal arch within an imaginary landscape; ink and bistre wash drawing (Paris, Archives nationales).

Napoleon I nurtured an ambition to transform the capital of his empire into the most beautiful city in the world. On 17 February 1806, plans for a "column dedicated to the glory of the Grande Armée" (presently the Place Vendôme column) were confirmed definitively. On 18 February, an Imperial decree approved the completion of the Pantheon and the "erection of a triumphal arch at the entry to the boulevard near the site of the former Bastille prison, in such a way that, upon entering the Saint-Antoine district, one passed through this triumphal arch." During the following days, decisions were taken to construct the Iéna Bridge, the Stock Exchange, and the Carrousel Triumphal Arch at the Tuileries Palace. The choice of Place de la Bastille for the arch appeared compelling. Firstly, it gave a monumental eastern entrance into Paris. Secondly, on the very same historic site where the former monarchy had been symbolically abolished, it served as the inception of a grand Avenue which Napoleon dreamed of piercing through to the East colonnade of the Louvre. Lastly, the proposed arch permitted, in an implicit manner, the stifling of Revolutionary memories.

In March, architect Jean-François-Thérèse Chalgrin (1739-1811) was hired to study the best possible site for the arch. He took note of inconveniences at the Bastille: the public space did not have a precise form; the adjoining public roads were irregular; and the proposed east-west axis contravened the existing northern boulevard (presently Boulevard Richard Lenoir) which, due to its width, tended to impose its existing orientation onto the site. On the contrary, Place de la Concorde (formerly Place Louis V) offered, among other advantages, an already established,

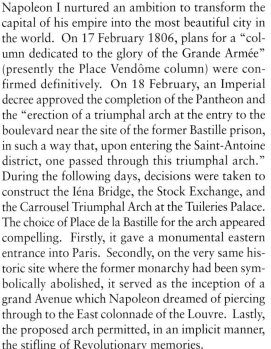

Chalgrin's autograph (Bibliothèque historique de la Ville de Paris).

Following double page: **Aerial views of the Place de l'Étoile and the Arc de Triomphe de l'Étoile:** to the west toward La Défense along the Avenue de la Grande-Armée; to the east toward the Tuileries and Palais du Louvre along the Avenue des Champs-Élysées.

Chalgrin and
Raymond's
projects inspired
by the Arch of
Titus in Rome;
watercolour and
gouache drawings
by Thierry (Paris,
Bibliothèque
historique de la
Ville de Paris).

♦ Pier:
*a solid masonry
support rising
vertically, from
which springs an
arch of an arcade
or a vault.*

♦ Entablature:
*the upper part of
a monument,
comprising
architrave♦, frieze,
and cornice.*

♦ Attic:
*the horizontal
storey or crown
above the main
entablature.*

♦ Architrave:
*a beam or lowest
division of the
entablature carried
by the column
capitals below.*

♦ Inscription:
*engraved words to
recall the memory
of an event or
person(s).*

graded layout which permitted easy accommodation of a new monument. On 9 May, Napoleon finally accepted an alternative site: Place de l'Étoile.

The Chalgrin-Raymond Partnership

On 11 May 1806, without any public competition, the project commission was entrusted to architects Chalgrin and Jean-Arnaud Raymond (1742-1811). The first stone was laid on 15 August 1806 to coincide with the Emperor's birthday. Chalgrin and Raymond submitted various schemes to a commission. Several distinguished personalities of the architectural world, including Antoine-Chrysostome Quatremère de Quincy (1755-1849), Charles Percier (1764-1838), Alexandre-Théodore Brongniart (1739-1813), and, of course, Pierre-François-Léonard Fontaine (1762-1853), First Architect to the Emperor, offered their opinions. In 1807, a first working project was established: by its size, the arch was to surpass all other contemporary constructions so as to be perfectly legible from Place de la Concorde and the Tuileries Palace. The choice of the Arch of Titus as an inspirational model alluded to Imperial Rome, pandering to the Emperor's taste for Antiquity. On the principal facade, a single arch was flanked by two massive piers♦ on which stood pairs of disengaged columns supporting an entablature♦. Above, at the attic♦ storey, each column was surmounted by a statue. Exposed wall surfaces were covered with inscriptions♦ or sculpted reliefs. In distinction to its antique model, a secondary arch opened onto the lateral facades.

From the moment the foundations were laid, criticism poured in. On 3 March 1808, Napoleon convened a special council (to which Fontaine was invited) to consider civic improvements to Paris. Concerning the Arc de Triomphe de l'Étoile, the Emperor's architect pronounced himself in favour of maintaining a single arch, insisted upon the perfect symmetry of all four facades, and questioned the real need for the presence of columns on the arch. Although the Emperor sided with Fontaine, he also opted for a general reduction of proportions and for a dimination of the emphasis on sculpture. However, as original foundations related to the first plan were too far advanced, modifications were not possible without engaging in difficult, expensive work. Because Chalgrin and Raymond could neither further enlarge the lateral facades, nor reduce the opening of the main arch, the architects proposed to restrict the height and length of the principal facades and to enlarge the transverse arch. That decision allowed them to create identical openings for the two arches, but to narrow the piers on the lateral facades. By the end of March, their design was presented to the Emperor and received his approval.

Jean-Arnaud Raymond; engraving by Charles Normand (Paris, Bibliothèque historique de la Ville de Paris).

Chalgrin's Arch

By a decree of 31 October 1808, the Administration appointed Chalgrin as the sole architect responsible for the monument. He elaborated a new plan which

Two of the bas-reliefs of the model of the Triumphal Arch built to mark the occasion of Marie-Louise's entry into Paris: *The Emperor's Clemency* and *The Embellishment of Paris;* engravings by Normand.

♦ **Spandrel:** a masonry detail forming a corner whose triangular space is enclosed by the curve of an arch, the horizontal line through its apex, and the vertical of its springing.

♦ **Projection:** an advancing bulge or jutting profile which interrupts a vertical plan.

♦ **Arcade:** an opening in the form of an arch, the ensemble comprising an arch (or range of arches) and its mounts or pressure points.

♦ **Course:** a range of stones laid horizontally to construct a wall.

♦ **Impost:** the projecting moulding surmounting a pier or a pillar of an arcade, on which the end of an arch rests.

♦ **Caisson:** the sunken panels or coffers in a ceiling, ornamented with mouldings.

♦ **Rosette:** a rose-shaped symmetrical ornament made by inscribed curves in a circle.

♦ **Cornice:** the cap or crown moulding forming an ornamental projection along the top of a building, wall, arch, or pedestal.

♦ **Pedestal:** a support or stylobate for one or more columns consisting of a base, die, and projecting cornice or cap moulding.

recalled proportions of the first proposal, but which removed the columns. On 27 March 1809, the monument was finally ready to be constructed according to his plans. Refined progressively until 1810, Chalgrin's drawings provided the definitive framework for the design of the arch until its completion twenty-six years later. The elevations facing Paris and Neuilly were based upon a simple geometric scheme: a square in which the central opening and the piers formed three seemingly equal vertical bands, topped by a massive horizonal plane (entablature and attic) which balanced with the mass of the piers. It would be difficult to imagine achieving an appearance of greater stability and harmony, perceived from afar. Chalgrin's ornamentation plan was simple: large, unadorned surfaces on which appeared sculpted, relief decoration within restricted zones. Four groups at the base of the piers were dedicated to the glory of all armies. In the upper section, six bas-reliefs narrated the emperor's battles. Victories featured in the spandrels♦ of the arch. In one statement, the monument celebrated the emperor himself, the Grande Armée, Austerlitz, and other great victories. In 1810, Chalgrin had the unexpected good fortune to see his drawings realized in full scale on the occasion of the marriage of Napoleon and Marie-Louise von Hapsburg. A wood and painted canvas replica of the Arc de Triomphe de l'Étoile (as it was to be built) was mounted in record time. This ceremonial decor allowed Chalgrin to make last minute corrections to the general composition, involving the reduction of attic proportions and the creation of projections♦ to give greater emphasis to the arcade♦ recessed in relation to the lateral sections. In 1811, Louis-Robert Goust (Chalgrin's former pupil) was named architect of the arch. He had previously served as First Inspector of the building site. By the end of 1813, already 19 metres high, the monument awaited the stone course♦ which was to carry the impost♦ of the great arch. Part of the sculpted ornaments had already been executed on the caissons♦ and rosettes♦ of the minor arch and on the cornice♦ of the pedestals.♦

Return of the Bourbons

In April 1814 imperial defeat and invasion halted work on the arch. Troops charged with the defence of Paris requisitioned wood from its scaffolding, while the summit of its solid masonry blocks was used as an observation post to survey enemy movements. Under the First Restoration, construction of

Huyot and Fontaine's plans; watercolour and gouache drawings by Thierry (Paris, Bibliothèque historique de la Ville de Paris).

such symbolic architecture no longer seemed appropriate. In May 1814, architect Bernard Poyet (1742-1824) went so far as to demand its destruction in order to erect a column which he had already proposed to Napoleon—but this time surmounted by a statue of Saint Louis. In 1818, at the beginning of the Second Restoration, there was a suggestion (without success) to transform the solid masonry blocks into a colossal fountain or to incorporate them into plans for some sort of colonnaded temple, dedicated to great kings and illustrious men of France. By an edict of 9 October 1823, Louis XVIII decreed that "the Arc de Triomphe de l'Étoile be terminated immediately" to perpetuate the memory of courage, discipline, and bravery of the Army of the Pyrenees in Spain, led by Louis-Antoine de Bourbon, duc d'Angoulême, his nephew. On the 29th of the same month, work resumed. In a meeting of January 1824, however, the Conseil général des bâtiments civils severely criticized Chalgrin's composition, in particular the recession of the central arch.

Antiquity according to Huyot

On 19 August 1824, the architect Jean-Nicolas Huyot (1780-1840) was commissioned to modify Chalgrin's plans. Huyot had returned from an extensive Mediterranean voyage devoted to the study of antique remains. Based upon this archaeological tour (apparently sufficient to establish his notoriety), he presented an interpretation of the Arch of Septimus Severus, a scheme which doubled the scale of its model, and coiffed the structure with a crown featuring France triumphant, in a chariot drawn by eight horses. This proposal required a modification to the existing solid

Jean-Nicolas Huyot; lead pencil drawing by Heim, 1829 (Paris, Musée du Louvre).

masonry blocks and the attachment of columns there to frame the bas-reliefs and military trophies. Generally approved by the Conseil des bâtiments civils at the start, the new design ran counter to the opinion formerly pronounced against the establishment of the columns and would have meant destroying half of each side of the arch, as well as reopening the foundations, an operation judged risky and extravagant. By an order of 12 May 1825, Charles X decided that Chalgrin's plans would be followed (apart from certain improvements) without altering the general composition which had been adopted on 27 March 1809. Fontaine also declared himself in favour of carrying on with the work according to Chalgrin's drawings, dashing Huyot's last hopes. A royal order of 3 December 1825 charged Guy de Gisors (1762-1835), General Inspector of Public Works and Chalgrin's former pupil, to oversee the destruction of non-conforming elements according to terms set forth in the 12 May edict. On 16 December, the Minister of the Interior removed Huyot from office for having refused to comply with orders.

Fontaine;
oil on canvas
by Joseph-Desiré
Court
(Compiègne,
Musée national
du Château).

Fontaine's Plan

Invited to replace Huyot, Fontaine declined. Instead, he suggested handing over the building works to a commission presided over by himself, Gisors (assisted by Percier), and Étienne-Éloy de La Barre (1764-1833), Percier's pupil. The commission entrusted Fontaine with the drafting of the final plan. The so-called heresy of the recessed central arch was corrected by continuing on the projections right up to the entablature and attic. The totality of the central portion of each side, and not simply the arcade, was to appear recessed as well. A high circular pedestal, supporting a sculptural group, also topped the central section, while each bay within the piers was surmounted by an equestrian figure. Divided and laden with ornaments, the attic no longer served as the horizontal link. It became the dominant vertical, accentuated by a complex crown, thereby endowed with greater importance. The iconography♦ of the monument was totally modified to emphasize specific political allegories alluding to benefits afforded by the restoration of peace. In January 1827, the commission drew up a preliminary list of sculptors from whom they requested sketches. But Huyot, profiting from the fall of the Villèle Ministry on 3 January 1828, was restored to his post. The commission's own members were dismissed without further ado.

♦ **Iconography:**
a group of figural
representations
illustrating an estab-
lished subject.

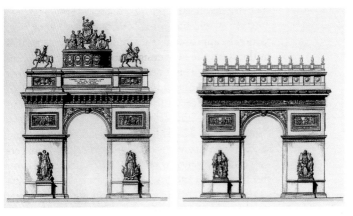

Huyot's Return

To resume his post, Huyot was obliged neither to destroy anything in the exisiting scheme, nor to engage in modifications which would increase general expenditures. The architect decided to slow down construction to give himself more time to redesign the upper sections in his own style. After having fought so hard against Chalgrin's original project, he partially reverted to it by suppressing projections at the entablature and attic level, initially instigated by the Fontaine-Gisors commission. Huyot decorated the entablature with a figurative frieze♦—quite similar to Chalgrin's ornamental frieze design—substituting the series of consoles♦ conceived by Fontaine. As for the attic, he covered it with an alternating rhythm of pilasters♦ and shields, surmounted by a marvellous suite of statues representing the cities of France, whose pedestals were joined by a balustrade. If the concept was original, the iconography proved rather conventional. In order to arrange for models of decorative details on the Étoile arch, Huyot obtained permission to have casts made of ornaments on the Roman Arch of Titus. In particular, he commissioned the execution, after these models, of the Fames set in the spandrels of the great arches, a job he entrusted to sculptor James Pradier, after having considered Jean-Pierre Cortot. Following the July 1830 Revolution, the building works profited from the labour of a charity workshop which was set up at the arch. One of the first gestures of King Louis-Philippe (who, as the former duc d'Orléans, owed much of his reputation for liberalism to his presence at Général Dumouriez's side at Valmy and Jemmapes) was to reaffirm the dedication of the monument to the armies of the Revolution and Empire. Due to Huyot's habitual, constant, and erratic performances which had grown quite serious, the architect was dismissed on 20 July 1832. On 31 July, Guillaume-Abel Blouet (1795-1853) replaced him.

Project by the Gisors-Percier-La Barre-Debret commission, and Huyot's drawing of his own modifications to his initial project; engravings.

♦ **Frieze:** an ornamental border forming a continuous band immediately below the cornice of the entablature.

♦ **Console:** a projecting moulding or bracket in the shape of a volute or 'S', serving as a support.

♦ **Pilaster:** a shallow, engaged pier (or rectangular column) projecting only slightly from a wall.

Abel Blouet; engraved medallion.

Completion by Blouet

The new chief architect set out to conform very faithfully to his predecessor's design: with the attic rid of its proposed balustrade and statues on the crown, construction resumed. Meanwhile, at the same attic level, Blouet reestablished the interior of the monument with its great vaulted hall, first planned by Chalgrin and abandoned by Huyot. This vaulting had been conceived to function not as a support for the crown, but rather as a large, technical platform for the storage of fireworks and other illuminations. According to Chalgrin's wishes, the hall itself was to have served as a museum. This was achieved in 1834. Blouet proposed to decorate it with a fresco whose principal subject (painted in grisaille) represented France distributing Wreaths to the Victors. The work was only partially finished when a decision was taken to halt proceedings.

The exterior of the monument owes very little to Blouet. Last in the line of architects, he accentuated, above all, the tendency of his predecessors to multiply its ornaments. Thus, he had the attic pilasters sculpted with a motif of double-edged swords. In 1835, he broke up the severity of the straight cornice by surmounting it with a ridge (doubling as guard rail) decorated with Medusa heads linked by an alternating motif of antique shields and palmettes. And ultimately, it was Blouet himself who was responsible for the building site at the moment when the decision was taken to execute the great sculptural ensembles of 1833-1836. He retained the idea of the large trophies, but gave them as theme the 'moving forces' of society: a figure of Mars personifying War; Minerva, the Arts and Sciences; Mercury, Commerce; and Ceres, Agriculture.

The Dream of a Crown

Jules-Denis Thierry; first inspector of the arch from 1824; medallion (Paris, Bibliothèque historique de la Ville de Paris).

On 27 April 1834, then acting Minister of the Interior Adolphe Thiers (1797-1877) took the decision to have the arch crowned. Blouet was immediately charged with establishing a pedestal for this operation, and the most important sculptors of the period —Pradier, Antoine-Louis Barye— were invited to submit designs on the theme of a symbolic eagle. In 1838, *France Victorious* was executed in plaster after a maquette by Gabriel-Bernard Seurre (1795-1867). Although well received, this composition (6.5 metres high) was replaced in 1840 by a group designed by Blouet, adhering more closely to the theme of a national homage to the Eagle's return. In 1853, Jean-

Auguste Barre (1811-1896) presented a scheme for *The Equestrian Triumph of Napoleon*. The arch was centred within a circle composed of statues of Imperial marshals. In 1882, Alexandre Falguière (1831-1900) proposed the last of the grand projects for the crowning of the arch. That same year, he exhibited a maquette of a quadriga carrying the Republic, seated, holding the national flag and the *Declaration of the Rights of Man*. She was accompanied by workers symbolizing civic duty and by a soldier dying in action next to his comrade in battle, symbols of military duty. The work received great critical acclaim: the Commission of the 14 July celebrations decided to a life-size plaster replica to install in situ to judge its impact. Although the trial proved not altogether convincing, the plaster model remained in place until 1886, inclement weather having gradually whittled it away. All other ideas to crown the arch were subsequently abandoned.

Gabriel-Bernard Seurre's scheme for an equestrian group; watercolour and gouache drawing by Thierry, 1838 (Paris, Musée d'Orsay).

The Inauguration

On 29 July 1830, Thiers, as President of the Council, and the comte d'Argout, as Minister of Finance, inaugurated the monument to commemorate the sixth anniversary of the Trois Glorieuses (July 27-29). Grandiose festivities originally planned were cancelled: Louis-Philippe feared an assassination attempt and sought to avoid offending foreign chancelleries likely to be irked by the memory of events celebrated on the walls of the arch. Throughout the day, an immense crowd gathered amidst the playing of Revolutionary and Imperial military airs. By evening, the arch was illuminated by gaslight specially set up for the occasion. In addition to candelabras installed along the perimeter of the monument, a cord was strung around the entire entablature, fed by seven hundred gas lamps. Still more extraordinary, thirty-six festoons♦, terminal points on the attic, were crowned by bouquets linked by a garland which meandered along the sinuous lines of the architecture. The entire structure was illuminated by approximately one thousand lamps, the gas originating from the neighbouring Ternes factory.

From the Return of the Ashes...

On 15 December 1840, over 400,000 people witnessed the return of Napoleon I's ashes. His coffin was placed on a catafalque adorned with twelve caryatids, borne in a funeral chariot drawn by twelve black horses caparisoned in gold. Hundreds of men escorted the convoy. The stretch of road was bordered by columns surmounted by Imperial eagles, smoking torches, and standing figures of French historical figures who appeared to constitute a formidable, hieratic guard of honour. Once arrived beneath the arch, the catafalque came to a halt. An immense cry resounded from the assembled crowd: "Long live the Emperor!" On 20 April 1848, three days before organized general elections following the overthrow of Louis-Philippe, a gigantic Fête de la Fraternité et du Printemps de la jeune IIe République (Festival of Brotherhood and Spring of the Second Republic) reunited all Paris on the Champs-Élysées. The arch served as a solemn framework for a grand, ceremonial construction whose steps rose almost to the height of the imposts of the minor arches. Lower down, at the level of Rude and Cortot's sculptural groups, was established a vast esplanade with tribunal stations to which led a monumental staircase. It was there, in the presence of France's provisional government, presided over by astronomer-physician François Arago, that Republican flags were presented to the regiments of the army and national guard.

♦ *Festoon:* a carved architectural ornament in the form of a swag or garland of flowers and fruit, suspended at both ends in a loop.

... to the Commune

The Second French Republic vanished with a coup d'état on 2 December 1851, orchestrated by its first and only elected president, Prince Louis-Napoleon Bonaparte. Henceforth, every 15 August, Napoleon I's birthdate, the arch, bathed in light, surmounted by the emperor's name and crown, found itself the focus of one of the most important dynastic celebrations. In 1853, the architect Jacques-Ignace Hittorff (1792-1867) proposed the creation of a square (320 metres in diameter) prolonging the Neuilly side of the arch by a vast, rectangular esplanade. Devoid of all vegetation, this unified design was bordered by blocks of flats inspired by those along the Rue de Rivoli. The place included two monumental, symmetrical portals, one facing Chaillot, the other Roule. Ultimately, in 1854, a less ambitious project was adopted. The square was reduced to a simple circle (262 metres in diameter) planted with four ranges of trees from which twelve large avenues radiated. Around the border of the square, sumptuous mansions were oriented, each fronting upon a garden. Facades were decorated with Corinthian pilasters, garlands, and laurel wreaths, discreet allusions to Imperial Rome. A pattern of candelabras in the shape of a stack of swords harmonized with the grillwork of neighbouring mansions. In 1860, Ledoux's two tollgate pavilions located on the place were destroyed. The development was completed in 1869.

Hardly had the Place de l'Étoile been terminated when, unexpectedly, the Empire collapsed and the Prussians invaded. If the monument suffered little during the Prussian bombardments, civil war scarcely spared it. During the siege of Paris by government troops, Communal federates managed to hoist five guns onto the platform at night. Unlimbered, this artillery battery fired no fewer than fifty shells during the single day of 10 April 1871, provoking such vibrations in the structure that the Communards ceased firing and contented themselves with using the summit as an observation post. On the Neuilly side, Antoine Etex's sculptural group was badly damaged because the sand bags and hoardings which had protected the sculptures during the Prussian invasion had been too rapidly disengaged at the end of the conflict.

Destruction of Ledoux's tollgate pavilions in 1860; engraving (Paris, Bibliothèque nationale de France).

Barricades in front of the west facade facing Avenue de la Grande-Armée; anonymous photograph, 1871 (Paris, Bibliothèque nationale de France).

First aerial view of the Arc de Triomphe taken from a captive balloon, south-west direction: to the left, Avenue de l'Impératrice, presently Avenue Foch; photograph by Félix Tournachon, called Nadar, 1868 (Paris, Médiathèque du patrimoine).

Victor Hugo's catafalque, 22 May 1885; the arch is surmounted by a plaster-cast quadriga from *The Triumph of France* by Alexandre Falguière; anonymous photograph (Paris, Musée Victor Hugo).

Victory Cenotaph installed at the top of Avenue des Champs-Élysées for the 14 July 1919 parade; Harlingue-Viollet photograph.

Victor Hugo's Funeral

On 22 May 1885, aged 83, Victor Hugo passed away, not far from the very arch which he so often praised. Both Chamber and Senate ordered a state funeral. The poet's body lay in state under the Arc de Triomphe at the top of a catafalque, 22 metres high, designed by Charles Garnier, architect of the Paris Opéra. Departing from Falguière's equestrian group and veiling the figure of France herself, a simple, black crêpe veil draped the left side of the monument. Situated at the four corners of the platform, immense tricolour oriflammes at half-mast echoed the majestic flagpoles installed on the ground. Perfuming pans on pedestals replaced customary boundary stones. At the lateral sides of the monument, gigantic medallions framed portraits of the poet. All around the square, among the flag stack fasces, escutcheons bearing the titles of the author's great works were suspended from candelabras. On 29 May, eve of the funeral, several thousand persons gathered; on the following day, the funeral itself took place. Three days previously, the Chamber had decided to confer definitively to the Church of Sainte-Geneviève its destiny as national Pantheon and there to dispose the body of Victor Hugo.

Victory Parade

On 13 July 1919, a ceremony paid tribute to the one and a half million combatants who perished during the Great War. Under the grand arch was installed an immense cenotaph♦ whose four sides displayed Victory winged with aerofoils of a plane. The work of architect Louis Sue, decorator André Mare, and painter Gustave Jaulmes, this stupendous monument, 17.5 metres high and over 8 metres wide, weighed more than 30 tons. Plaster-cast and gilded, the work had been executed in only ten days and nights by a team of forty-five craftsmen under the direction of sculptor Antoine Sartorio. As Clemenceau had decided at the very last minute that troops would pass under the arch, this enormous mass was moved to the entrance of the Champs-Élysées during the early morning hours. On 14 July, one thousand invalids crossed through the arch. Then, mounted on horseback at the head of their troops, the marshals of France led off the military parade from the Porte Maillot to the round-about of the Champs-Élysées. Behind them, the inter-Allied État-Major participated in the triumph. There followed the Japanese, Greek, Portuguese, Roumanian, Serbian, Croatian, Slovenian, Polish, and Czech regiments, and, finally, the French Army led by Marshal Pétain. At the head of these regiments, some bedraggled standards bore the tragic names of the battles of Aronne, Douaumont, Marne, Meuse, and Verdun.

♦ *Cenotaph: a monument elevated in memory of the dead buried elsewhere.*

22 | **Arrival of the Unknown Soldier under the arch, 28 January 1921;** Viollet photograph.

Humoristic postcard published during the war of 1914-1918, parodying the group in *La Marseillaise* with uniforms of diverse armies (Paris, Collection Cl. Malécot).

The Unknown Soldier

From 1916, an idea developed to open the doors of the Pantheon to "one of the unknown soldiers who died valiantly for his country" on whose tomb would be inscribed two words, "A Soldier", and two dates, "1914-191?". Espoused in 1918 and supported by a fervent press campaign, the proposition was ultimately accepted. On 12 November 1919, the Chamber of Deputies decided that the anonymous remains of the French soldier killed in combat would be transferred to the Pantheon. Meanwhile, associations of former combatants challenged the choice of the site, preferring to affirm the exceptional character of this death, symbol of the hundreds of thousands of others killed in action. The author Binet-Valmer led a virulent campaign to entomb this unknown soldier under the Arc de Triomphe. On 8 November 1920, the deputies unanimously voted in a law, equally approved unanimously by the Senate, which awarded the honours of the Pantheon "to the remains of one of the unknown soldiers killed in action during the 1914-1918 war". At three o'clock in the afternoon on 10 November 1920, in a blockhouse at the Verdun citadel transformed into a chapel, a young infantryman laid down a bouquet of flowers (gathered from the battlefield of Verdun) on one of eight identical coffins brought back from different zones at the Front: Flanders, Artois, the Somme, Île-de-France, Chemin-des-Dames, Champagne, Verdun, Lorraine. On 11 November, the tank transporting Léon Gambetta's heart and the gun carriage bearing the unknown soldier's remains rejoined the Arc de Triomphe. The catafalque of the Unknown Soldier was lifted into one of the interior chambers of the edifice. A permanent guard was organized until the final inhumation on 28 January 1921 at the centre point of the principal arch facing upon the Champs-Élysées. In the presence of British Prime Minister Lloyd George, Marshals Foch, Joffre, and Pétain, and all the government, the Minister of War Louis Barthou laid down the Legion of Honour, the Military Medal, and the Military Cross on the tricolour flag covering the coffin, in "supreme homage from the country to the humble and anonymous heroes who fell for her". Following this ceremony, the Unknown Soldier was at last placed in his tomb.

Postcard published in 1921 on the occasion of the burial of the Unknown Soldier (Paris, Collection Cl. Malécot).

Detail of the shield adorning the inlet of the Memorial Flame, designed by architect Henri Favier and executed in 1923 by iron craftsman Edgar Brandt.

Memorial Flame

Two years after the inhumation of the Unknown Soldier, journalist and poet Gabriel Boissy launched the idea of a Memorial Flame, which immediately received enthusiastic public approbation. With active support from André Maginot (then Minister of War), Léon Bérard (Minister of State Education), and Paul Léon (Director of Fine Arts), the project advanced rapidly. Edgar Brandt, a wroughtiron craftsman, was selected to execute the torch, designed by architect Henri Favier: a circular bronze shield at the centre of which opened a cannon muzzle from which radiated a frieze of swords. On 11 November 1923, surrounded by a multitude of former combatants, Maginot ignited the flame for the first time. Since that moment, the flame has never been extinguished. A daily ritual pays tribute to the Great Dead: each evening, at six-thirty, a flame is rekindled by one of the nine hundred associations of former combatants regrouped under the association La Flamme sous l'Arc de Triomphe. During the Occupation, this daily kindling rite was performed unperturbed. On 26 August 1944 at three o'clock in the afternoon, before descending triumphantly down the Champs-Élysées within liberated Paris, General Charles de Gaulle came to lay down the white-flowered Cross of Lorraine on the Tomb of the Unknown Soldier. Since then, the Arc de Triomphe has provided the framework for all great national celebrations: 11 November, 8 May, and, of course, the national fête of 14 July.

D.F. and G.P.

General de Gaulle placing a spray of flowers on the tomb of the Unknown Soldier, 26 August 1944, in liberated Paris (Paris, Musée d'Histoire contemporaine).

Visit

Epopee

In 1833, during a speech before the Chamber of
Deputies to vote in the budget, Thiers justified Louis-
Philippe's decision to complete the triumphal arch
in the name of the armies of the Republic and the
Empire, by declaring: "Arriving after forty years of
political trials of all sorts, this government has established its goal to resume, complete, and consolidate
all institutions which had been tested previously. It
would be consistent and preferable, therefore, in
assuming large-scale projects, to complete works
already begun than to initiate new ones." Louis-
Philippe resumed the construction of the triumphal
arch by renewing Napoleon's intentions: to show
his gratitude to the armies of the Empire without
forgetting to include therein those of the Revolution.
This gesture proved that he did not reject
Revolutionary values, memories of which had been

**Ornaments on
the entablature
and great
vault;** wash,
gouache, and
watercolour by
Thierry (Paris,
Bibliothèque
historique de la
Ville de Paris).

ORNEMENTS DE L'ENTABLEMENT ET DE LA GRANDE VOUTE.

François Rude; Pierre Petit photograph (Paris, Musée d'Orsay).

Jean-Pierre Cortot; oil on canvas by Ingres (Paris, Musée du Louvre).

Antoine Etex; Nadar photograph, 1876 (Paris, Médiathèque du patrimoine).

James Pradier; pastel on paper by Jean-François Gigoux (Versailles, Musée national du Château et des Trianons).

a determinant force during the barricades of 30 July 1830. The arch had taken on the entire commission for the sculptural programme under the Restoration (initiated by architect Huyot) had to be modified. Thiers was charged with the task. An art critic and collector, he had a predilection for the Revolution, Consulate, and Empire (to which he devoted several books). All factors predisposed him to devote close attention to the edifice which was to glorify these periods. Its sculpture was executed between 1833 and 1836. If the chosen themes were obligatorily conventional, the selection of sculptors had to reflect as well the national spirit of the monument. This explains the presence of artists with classical tendencies (Cortot and Lemaire) and sculptors allied to new Romanticism (Etex, Gechter, Chaponnière, Marochetti, and Feuchère). Prestigious sculptors (such as Rude and Pradier) and young talents rubbed shoulders. Determined to be popular and to make the monument a genuine national and 'social' work place for unemployed sculptors, the Government parcelled out the commission among twenty-two artists. Critics deplored this lack of unity and regretted that Thiers had not confided the most important section to Rude, whose brilliant work surpassed all other sculpture on the arch. The Arc de Triomphe was one of the rare buildings of the July Monarchy to have accommodated so much Romantic sculpture. *The Battle of Jemmapes, The Battle of Austerlitz, Crossing the Arcole Bridge,* and *The Conquest of Alexandria* give evidence of a Romantic spirit which had played a role within the artistic avant-garde since 1820. Characters in perpetual disequilibrium and turbulent scenes constituted veritable snapshots: heroic drama was deemed worthy as the main subject of these sculptures. They perfectly translated the Romantic ideal: action and sacrifice as the means to combat blind forces of destiny. Other works manifested a more ambiguous character, drawing from Classical and Romantic tendencies, as witnessed in Etex's works, *The Resistance* and *Departure of the Volunteers,* the latter defying classification.

I.R.

The tour of the arch exterior begins in a northerly direction from the east facade and moves clockwise, according to the following order: lower and upper reliefs on the piers, spandrels, and frieze of the entablature.

The tour ends with the interior reliefs and spandrels and, finally, with the ground inscriptions.

Lower Reliefs on the Piers

East

Side facing Avenue des Champs-Élysées. Lower section of the north-east pillar.

| 29

Departure of the Volunteers, called *La Marseillaise*[1]

by François Rude (1784-1855)

The high relief♦ represents the Genius of Liberty in the guise of a winged female emitting a cry of warning in face of enemy invasion. She incites the people to battle by brandishing a sword. Beneath this figure, a bearded, breast-plated warrior leads along a naked youth by the shoulders, while waving his helmet to signal departure and unification. He seems indifferent to the advice apparently offered to him by a bearded old man in the background.

To the right, carrying a shield and draped in a coat, another warrior readies himself to follow his companions. To the left, a stooping soldier braces himself, while behind, a man wearing a helmet sounds the trumpet. A last soldier reins in a whinnying horse by his bridle. Rude illustrates a basic event in Revolutionary history: the conscription of 1792 which involved the levying of 200,000 men en masse under orders of the Legislative Assembly in order to organize the defence of France against foreign armies allied against the Revolutionaries. This massive conscription had secured

♦ **High relief:** a sculpted relief whose projecting forms represent more than half the volume of the object represented.

***La Marseillaise,
detail:*** the
bearded cuirassier
and naked young
man parting for
battle.

the first victory of the
Revolution against a foreign
power: the Battle of Valmy
against Prussia on 20 September
1792. A short while after, on
6 November 1792, the
Revolutionary armies won a
second memorable battle
against Austria, at Jemmapes.
In confronting the enemy, the
Nation unified. Thus it was
obvious to celebrate that
conscription in a monument
which aspired to be national.
If Rude represented a real
episode in the history of France,
he nonetheless treated his
subject in an allegorical manner:
he employed neither costumes
of the epoch, nor contemporary
Revolutionary arms.

Instead, the upper relief strives
to achieve a universal dimension
and to symbolize the struggle
of a people, whomever they be,
in defence of their territory.

Napoleon's Triumph[2]

by Jean-Pierre Cortot
(1787-1843)

Crowned by Victory, Napoleon is represented in antique vestments, pressing a sword against his chest. In the background to the right, a profiled kneeling man symbolizes a prisoner enchained at the feet of his victor. To the left, the allegory of a city, with a crenellated crown, kneels before the conqueror whose protective hand extends over her. Behind, the Muse of History inscribes on a tablet the memorable events of Napoleon's reign.

Above, sounding a trumpet and bearing a standard, winged Fame soars across a palm tree, an image evoking the Egyptian expedition. This scene is meant to illustrate the year 1810, date of the apogee of Napoleon's reign: his marriage with Marie-Louise of Austria to assure the future of the dynasty, and conquests which expanded the Empire to its maximum. Cortot's Fame serves as pendant to Rude's Genius of Liberty. The sculptor David d'Angers commented on the work: "Cortot's sculpture is icy. Its proportions, measurements, and limbs are flawless. Yet life itself, its soul, is missing."

Lower Reliefs on the Piers

West
Side facing Avenue de la Grande-Armée. Lower section of the south-west pillar.

The Resistance[3]
by Antoine Etex
(1808-1888)

This high relief symbolizes the Nation's resistance in 1814 when faced with the invasion of foreign forces united against Napoleon. The Russians and Austrians had invaded French territory and occupied the capital. Resistance to invasion perfectly represents the national theme: faced with the enemy, all domestic differences must be obliterated so that the Nation regains its cohesion and its capacity to preserve its territorial independence. With left fist clenched and right hand armed with a double-edged sword, a standing nude warrior readies himself to leave in defence of his native land. To his right, his aged father holds him back by the leg.

To his left, holding their child in her outstretched arms, his wife, too, attempts to retain him. Behind this warrior, a bearded horseman falls from his saddle as though struck down in full action symbolizing a patriot's sacrifice for his country. Wings deployed and forehead bearing a flame, with sword in his right hand and left fist clenched, the Spirit of the Future dictates to the soldier his duty to resist.

Lower Reliefs on the Piers

West

Side facing Avenue
de la Grande-Armée.
Lower section
of the north-west pillar.

| 33

Peace[4]

by Antoine Etex

This relief represents the return of peace after the Treaty of Paris in 1815 which brought an end to Napoleon's attempt to return to power during the One Hundred Days. It constitutes a logical pendant to The Resistance. At the centre of the composition, a mother holds her child on her knees. Near her, a young boy is engrossed in reading. To the left of the soldier, a kneeling peasant examines the cutting blade of his plough. Behind, a farm labourer tames a bull. Wearing a helmet and armed with a spear, Minerva dominates the composition as goddess of victory and inspiration to the arts and labours of peace. All fundamental social activities are reborn in peace time: agriculture can become prosperous again, the family reconstituted, and education flourishes once again.

East

Side facing Avenue
des Champs-Élysées.
Upper section
of the north-east
and south-east pillars.

The Obsequies of General Marceau[5]
by Henri Lemaire
(1798-1880)

One of the young heroes who sacrificed himself to the Revolution, General Marceau died at the Battle of Altenkirchen in 1796 at the head of the Sambre and Meuse army. He lies dead on a stretcher at the centre of the relief. To the left, accompanied by a group of four Austrian officers, Archduke Charles of Austria, head of the enemy army, places a crown on the body to render homage to him. To the right are featured some soldiers of the Sambre and Meuse army: one officer weeps on the chest of another who hides his eyes; a soldier leans on his rifle.

Detail of The Obsequies of General Marceau: Austrian officers gathering before the hero's remains.

The Battle of Aboukir[6]
by Gabriel-Bernard Seurre, called Seurre l'Aîné
(1795-1867)

During the Egyptian Campaign, Aboukir (a city not far from Alexandria, held by the French) was threatened by an Ottoman landing. Before having received reinforcements, Bonaparte launched an offensive. His heroic operation succeeded thanks to General Murat, who himself was captured as prisoner of Pasha Mustapha Kinceï, Supreme General of the Ottoman armies. At centre, an aide de camp presents Mustapha Kinceï to Bonaparte and General Murat. Some captives follow the Pasha. One of them prostrates himself before Bonaparte, whose horse strides across a cadaver and the debris of Ottoman arms.

Detail of The Battle of Aboukir: Bonaparte on horseback receiving the captives.

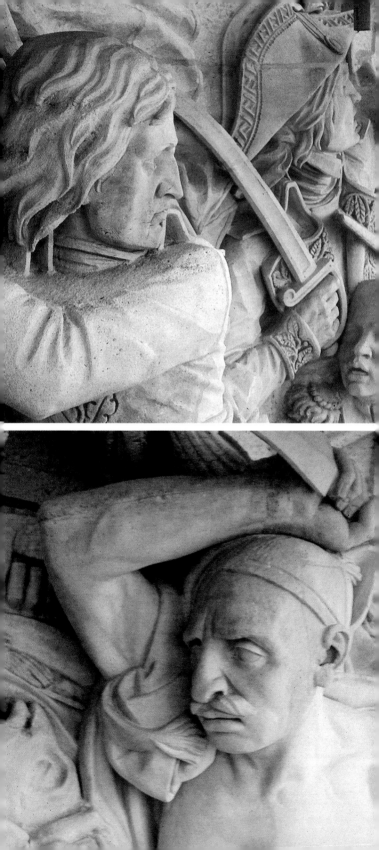

Upper Reliefs on the Piers

West

Side facing Avenue de la Grande-Armée. Upper section of south-west and north-west pillars.

| 37

Crossing the Arcole Bridge [7]

by Jean-Jacques Feuchère (1807-1852)

The episode of the Arcole Bridge crossing constitutes part of the illustrious battles of the Italian Campaign. With sword in one hand and tricolour flag in the other, Bonaparte crosses over the Arcole Bridge beyond which the Austrian troops are massing. Wounded in battle, General Muiron falls, attempting in vain to restrain Bonaparte. Behind the hero, soldiers follow his example, as does the young drummer, still a child, who flings himself after him. The general situated behind Bonaparte is Augereau, the true hero of this battle, for whom Bonaparte substitutes himself thanks to skilful propaganda.

Detail of Crossing the Arcole Bridge Bonaparte crossing the bridge, brandishing the tricolour flag.

The Conquest of Alexandria [8]

by John Chaponnière (1801-1835)

On 3 July 1798 during the Egyptian Campaign, General Kléber, followed by his soldiers, reached the summit of the Alexandrian ramparts. Wounded in the head, he holds his right hand to his forehead. With left hand armed with a sword, he points out the enemy to his troops. A French soldier pierces his bayonet into the chest of a Turk who injured Kléber, while a nude Egyptian prepares to stab this French soldier. Behind Kléber, a soldier rips his cartouche, as a second one mounts the last step which gives out onto the ramparts. To the left, one last soldier appeals to his companions.

Detail of The Conquest of Alexandria An Egyptian combatant prepares to stab a French soldier.

Lateral Upper Reliefs

North
Side facing Avenue de Wagram.
The Battle of Austerlitz

South
Side facing Avenue Kléber.
The Battle of Jemmapes

The Battle of Austerlitz[2]
by Théodore Gechter (1796-1844)

A mounted Napoleon occupies central position in the relief. Without stirring, he observes the struggle among the Russians, Austrians, and French infantry who charge with bayonnets. At his right, the Imperial Guard remains at a standstill, while to the left the fray breaks into a furious rage. Dismounting from his horse, General Friant forces

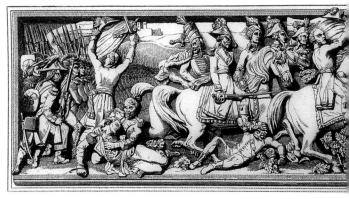

The Battle of Jemmapes[10]
by Charles Marochetti (1805-1868)

The central figure in this high relief is General Dumouriez mounted on a rearing horse, followed by Brigadiers Rosières, Ferrand, Stennebosse, Bloisières, and the duc de Chartres, future King Louis-Philippe. Dumouriez brandishes his hat to signal unification, as his troops seem momentarily hesitant. Behind him, General Drouet

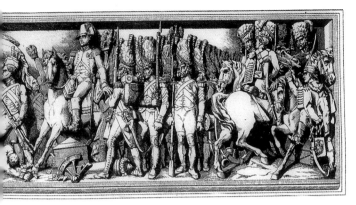

his way through at the same moment as the Russians and Austrians fall into Sokolnitz pond whose ice gives way beneath their feet. Bodies of those cavalrymen who have slid into the pond are only half-visible. On 2 December 1805, first anniversary of Napoleon I's coronation, victory was won.

(having broken his leg by falling from his horse) is tended by an ambulance officer.

Viewed from the rear, General Thouvenot rushes forward with raised sabre onto the enemy's flank.

In the right section of the relief, French infantry and Austrian cavalry are engaged in battle. Arm in a sling, an Austrian officer is taken prisoner, while a second man falls from his horse into the fray.

Details of *The Battle of Austerlitz:* Napoleon on horseback, two hussars of the cavalry, and Austrian soldiers.

Spandrels of the Major Arches

East
Side facing Avenue des Champs-Élysées.

West
Side facing Avenue de la Grande-Armée.

The Fames[11-12]
by James Pradier
(1790-1852)

James Pradier executed these two figures after plaster copies from the Arch of Titus commissioned by architect Huyot from the French Academy in Rome. The artist managed to reproduce these high reliefs much larger than the original ones: the latter measure less than 6 metres high. On the side facing Avenue des Champs-Élysées, each Fame blows a trumpet, while those facing Avenue de la Grande-Armée hold forth crowns.

The Fames by James Pradier: Allegorical figures in the central arch spandrels, west and east sides.

Spandrels of the Minor Arches

North
Side facing Avenue de Wagram.
The Infantry

South
Side facing Avenue Kléber.
The Cavalry

The Infantry[13]
by Théophile Bra
(1797-1863)

Two figures are represented in the spandrels: to the left, a grenadier; to the right, a chasseur.

The Cavalry[14]
by Étienne Valois
(1785-1862)

In the left spandrel, seen from the rear, a nude carabineer brandishes a sabre in his right hand. In the opposite spandrel, seen frontally, a lancer extends his right hand to seize his sabre.

Friezes on the Entablature

The Departure of the Armies

East

Side facing Avenue des Champs-Élysées and half of the lateral elevations.

Great Figures of the Revolution and the Empire[15]

by Sylvestre Brun

Before the altar of the Fatherland are assembled Desaix, the duc de Chartres, Masséna, Kléber, Houchard, Kellermann, Daboville, Lefebvre, Augereau, Gouvion-Saint-Cyr, Eugène and Joséphine de Beauharnais, David, Gossec, and Rouget de Lisle. From the centre to the extreme left of the scene on

Cavalrymen and Grenadiers[16]

by Charles-René Laitié (1782-1862)
(right section of the central motif, left section of the side elevation)

The Artillery is shown on the part of the lateral elevation facing Avenue de Wagram up to the central window.

Hussars and Sappers[17]

by Georges Jacquot (1794-1874)
(left section of the central motif, right section of the side elevation)

The Infantry is represented on the part of the frieze continuing from the elevation facing Avenue Kléber up to the central window.
A winged spirit is situated against the window and demarcates the end of the section executed by Jacquot.

the entablature are represented
Bailly, the duc d'Orléans, Sieyès,
La Fayette, Beurnonville,
Jourdan, Championnet, La Tour
d'Auvergne, Joubert, Cambronne,
Carnot, Soult, Hoche, Marceau,
Penthièvre, Madame Roland
and Monsieur Roland, Moitte,
and Chénier.

*Following
double page:*
**Cavalrymen and
grenadiers,** detail
of the north frieze
on the entablature,
east side of
*The Departure
of the Armies.*

Friezes on the Entablature

The Return of the Armies

West

Side facing Avenue de la Grande-Armée and half of the lateral elevations.

Allegory[18]

by Louis-Denis Caillouette (1790-1868)

Allegory is demarcated by two small triumphal arches. At the centre of the frieze, surrounded by Abundance and Peace, France distributes rewards to her victorious armies. Behind them is inscribed: "To its courageous, France is grateful". Cavalrymen

The Return of the Armies from Italy[19]

by Gabriel-Bernard Seurre, called Seurre the Elder

(right section of the central motif, left section of the side elevation)

A group of soldiers heads toward a triumphal arch on which is inscribed: "To the army from Italy". They escort a figure representing the Tiber River, recognizable as a she-wolf suckling Romulus and Remus set upon a float drawn by four horses. On the section which continues across the lateral

The Return of the Army from Egypt[20]

by François Rude

(left section of the central motif, right section of the side elevation)

A mass of people crossing through a triumphal arch advance upon army soliders from Egypt who bring home a sphinx on a chariot yoked to four bulls. Cuirassiers appear along half the lateral elevation facing Avenue de Wagram up to

18 **19** **20**

and soldiers, some wounded,
present themselves before the
figure of France to offer her
trophies from their victorious
campaign.

elevation to the side facing
Avenue Kléber, Seurre depicts
some wounded soldiers and an
Italian woman holding a child in
her arms who occupy seats on a
chariot hauled by oxen.

the central window. A wagon
carries the wounded, while a
genie in Egyptian garb engraves
hieroglyphics on an obelisk
commemorating the heroic
deeds of the army from Egypt.

Lateral south elevation on the side facing Avenue Kléber.
From bottom to top: in the spandrels of the minor arches, *The Cavalry* and, in the background, *The Navy;* in the upper relief, *The Battle of Jemmapes.*

Victory over the East[21]
by Walcher

At centre, Victory holds a palm in her right hand and, in her left, a marble tablet on which is inscribed names of Bonaparte's great Eastern battles: Alexandria, the Pyramids, Aboukir, Heliopolis. To the left, a standing genie attempts to lead away a second one who has just planted his flag in the ground, a sign of taking possession of conquered provinces. To the right, two frolicking genies hold each other by the hands. Several symbols of the Orient are sculpted: Turkish flags on a pole topped by a crescent, a crocodile, and pyramids.

Victory over the North[24]
by Astyanax-Scaevola Bosio (1793-1876)

Seated at centre, Victory holds a tablet on which she has inscribed : "Austerlitz/léna/ Friedland and Ulm/Wagram and Eylau".

Positioned at her right and left, four genies shoulder a long garland whose ends spill over with fruit.

The Navy[25]
by Charles-Émile Seurre, called Seurre the Younger (1798-1858)

Detail of *The Navy.*

Victory over the West[23]
by Jean Espercieux (1757-1840)

At centre, Victory extends her arms toward the military genies over whom she raises laurel branches. The genies carry a garland of entwined fruit and flowers, symbol of abundance.

To the left, a genie presents Victory with a broken sceptre; behind him is found a shield on which is engraved: "Jemmapes/Fleurus". Situated at the extreme right, a genie pays tribute to Victory with a shattered diadem. Near him are laid out some oars and an anchor on which is inscribed "Espercieux 1830".

Victory over the South[22]
by Antoine-François Gérard (1760-1843)

Seated at centre, in her right hand Victory holds a sceptre surmounted by an Imperial eagle and, in her other hand, a tablet on which are inscribed names of Bonaparte's great victories in Italy: Marengo, Rivoli, Arcole, Lodi. To the left, two genies compose a trophy out of captured arms. To the right appears Napoleon's bust on which a genie of sculpture puts on the finishing touches. Another genie crowns the emperor's head.

The Artillery[26]
by Joseph Debay (1779-1863)

Previous page:
Detail of The Artillery.

MANTOUE
TAGLIAMENTO
SEDIMAN
MONT THABOR
CHEBREISSE
BASSIGNANO
SAN GIULIANO
DIETIKON
MUTTA THAL
GENES

LE VAR
MONTEBELLO
LE MINCIO
CALDIERO
CASTEL FRANCO
RAGUSE
GAETE

Tablets of battles, sieges, and storming of cities, with names of generals who commanded the armies and army corps.

Commemorative Tablets

In 1835, anxious to respect one of Napoleon's wishes and to relieve the barren walls of the Arc de Triomphe, Blouet obtained permission from Thiers to have listed there the great names of the Revolution and the Empire. Names of battles were to be engraved in four groups of twenty-five on the interior faces of the piers of the grand arch and on the shields of the attic. Generals' names were to be placed on six tablets of sixteen names on the four interior faces of the small piers according to geographic zones where these officers had participated in army campaigns in the North, South, East, and West. Head of a special commission, Peer and Lieutenant General Baron Saint-Cyr-Nugues was charged with establishing the lists. On 20 February 1836, he presented three lists of names: thirty decisive victories for the shields of the attic, ninety-six less determining army feats for the piers, and three hundred and eighty-four generals corresponding to the categories established by Blouet. Names were

underlined, and each tablet embellished with heroes' decorations and Crosses of the Legion of Honour. On 29 July 1836, the unveiling of these lists—approved without modification—provoked a wave of complaints from a great many families wishing to find mention of a forgotten hero whose service record fully justified his accession to the "honours of the Arc de Triomphe." The announcement that all new complaints would be examined provoked about one hundred additional requests.

After four years of stalemate, under pressure from Marshal Soult, duc de Dalmatie, President of the Conseil du roi, and War Minister, Blouet ended up finding space on the piers for one hundred and eight more generals, divided into eight tablets with sixteen names, and for seventy-two neglected battles. At the same time the Marshal instituted a commission presided over by Marshal Oudinot, duc de Reggio, grand chancelier de la Legion of Honour. They arrived at a total of two hundred and thirty-three names of generals or comparable categories, and seventy more names of battles, largely outdistancing the number of additions envisaged by the architect. Blouet resigned himself to using the piers of the minor arches. In fact, two hundred and fifty-six names (rather than the two hundred and thirty-three requested) were added. Until May 1842, thirty-five new names were accepted.

On July 1852, more than a dozen new names were added to the tablets of glory. Between 1893 and 1895, six other requests were fulfilled. Appeals submitted in 1919 and 1929 were rejected.

Ground Inscriptions

Tomb of the Unknown Soldier and the Memorial Flame:
Here/Lies/a French/Soldier/Who Died/For His Country/1914-1918[27].

Since 1945, four inscriptions have been added to those which had been sealed into the pavement under the vault of the Arch to commemorate two symbolic days, as evoked by the following lines engraved in bronze:
on the side facing Avenue Kléber,
4 September 1870/Proclamation/of the/Republic[28];
and, opposite, on the side facing Avenue de Wagram,
11 November 1918/Return of Alsace/And of Lorraine/To France[29].

On the side of Avenue de la Grande-Armée, the memory of contemporary conflicts is recognized at centre:
To the Combatants of the Armies/To the Combatants of the Resistance/ Who Died for France/1939-1945[30];
Appeal of 18 June 1940[31];
to the right:
To the Combatants/Of Indochina/The Nation/Is Grateful[32];
to the left, the last of these inscriptions, solemnly unveiled in 1999:
To Those Who Died for France/During the Algerian War and/The Battles of Tunisia and Morocco/1952-1962[33].

Tomb of the Unknown Soldier.

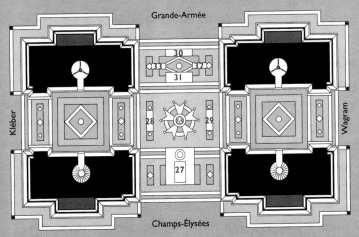

Grande-Armée

Kléber

Wagram

Champs-Élysées

The Halls

A first flight of stairs leads to rooms above the small lateral arches which serve to relieve their vaults. A second flight then mounts to a low-ceiling hall with pointed arches (39.84 metres long by 3.77 metres high) divided into three sections, situated under the principal arch at the entablature level. At present, this hall houses plaster casts of the four bas-reliefs (commissioned from Louis-Simon Boizot in 1799, executed in 1800) to decorate General Hoche's sarcophagus at Weissenthurm, entitled: *Attack on the Wissembourg Lines*, 28 December 1793; *The Capture of Fort Penthièvre at Quiberon*, 21 July 1795; *General Hoche's Pacification of the Vendée*, 1796; and *The Battle of Neuwied*, 18 April 1797. The original reliefs are conserved at the Musée de l'Histoire de France at the Château de Versailles. A much more spacious hall, with eliptical and semicircular vaults, has been converted under the terrace at the attic level to house the Musée de l'Arc. It contains a permanent exhibition of engravings, drawings, all types of original documents, photographs, and models, coinciding periodically with temporary expositions on the history of France. Bronze medals of world-

wide provenance entirely cover one wall of this hall; they were deposited in homage to the Unknown Soldier. The soldier at rest is the original plaster cast of the monument to the dead erected after World War I in the Cour du Mûrier at the École des Beaux-Arts in Paris. The terrace offers an exceptional view over Paris and its major east-west axis. It is also one of the rare places in the capital where one can observe the sky under full protection. At each summer solstice, the sun sets exactly in the axis of the grand arch. Exceeding Chalgrin's initial 1806 estimate by less than 200,000 francs, in spite of delays and slowdowns on the construction site, the arch cost 9,303,507 francs.

Arch Statistics

Overall monument
Height: 49.54 m
Length: 44.82 m
Width: 22.21 m

Vault of the grand arch
Height: 29.42 m
Width: 14.62 m

Vault of the minor arch
Height: 18.68 m
Width: 8.44 m

Sculpted groups in each pier
Height of figures: circa 5.85 m; 11.70 m, including their base.

Stairs
4, each comprised of 284 steps.

Elevator
Put into service in July 1929 in the north-west pillar of the arch; 20 person capacity (1,500 kg) over a circuit of 38 metres.

Materials
36,695 m³ of hewn stone and rubble, 128,000 kg of metal (rolled iron, cast iron, and lead).

Scaffolding
10,000 m³ of wood.

Total weight of monument, including foundations
Circa 100,000 tons.

Commemorative tablets
660 patronymics and 174 names of battles.

Previous page: **scaffolding system and cross section:** watercolour and gouache drawings by Thierry (Bibliothèque historique de la Ville de Paris).

Palm leaf from the Musée de l'Arc.

The Poilu Plaster model of a World War I French soldier (known as a *poilu*, or bearded one) by Jean Boucher for the monument to the dead at Vitré.

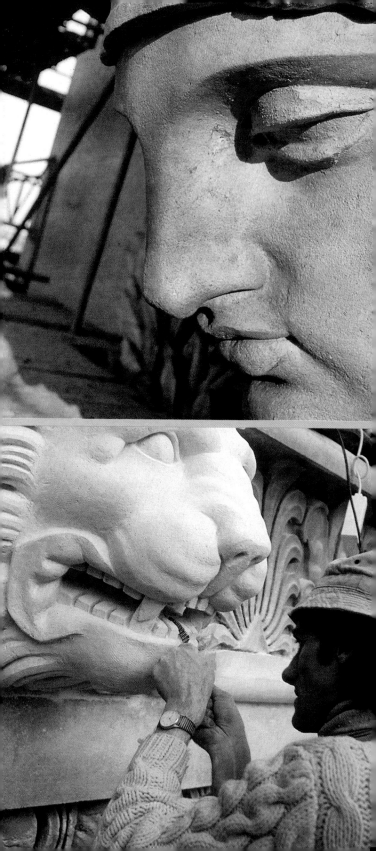

Restorations

After being seized as a target by the Versailles artillery in 1871, the arch was restored, above all on the Neuilly side. In 1896, a new campaign permitted repairing and cleaning. In 1944, violent Liberation battles inflicted serious damage to the arch, notably on the south facade. The frieze, entablature, modillions♦ and diverse sculpture, but also the structure, necessitated delicate restoration work. In 1965, efforts were made to erase the ravages of time, involving general cleaning and replacing numerous damaged stones, particularly on the sculptures.

Twenty years later, a stone which fell from the great arch signalled worrisome flaws in the masonry. Analysis revealed a series of fissures caused by pier settlement. Numerous constructions effectuated since 1965 on the north side of the place—the metro, RER, roadways, and underground pedestrian crossings—had modified the ancient drainage system for rainwater which flows under the foundations and eats into the mortar beds. From 1986 to 1989, under the direction of architect Michel Marot, a general campaign of consolidation was initiated, including selective injection of concrete and introduction of tie rods at the level of the vaulted rooms in the piers and the attic (in places where the edifice was hollow) to remedy the occurrence of spacing between walls. As this extensive structural (albeit nearly invisible) work was being carried out, an overall new cleaning protected the hewn stone of the arch from ambient pollutants. Under the direction of Catherine Feff, the scaffolding and protective netting metamorphosized into a gigantic tricoloured flag. A national fund financed half the building works which mounted to 34 million francs.

During the major restoration of 1989: Cleaning the central allegorical figure from the main group of *Peace*, and executing the lion's muzzle replica on the attic frieze.

Large, tricolour sheet covering the arch during the Bicentennial building works.

♦ **Modillion:** *a projecting and repetitive member, generally formed with ornamental scrolls or brackets, to support the weight of a cornice.*

Further Reading

Bercé, Françoise, "Napoléon architecte ou le goût historique," Les Monuments historiques de la France, n°4, October-December 1969, pp.25-57.

Damiron, Suzanne, "Projets de Chalgrin pour l'arc de triomphe de l'Étoile. Documents originaux," Urbanisme et architecture. Études écrites et publiées en l'honneur de Pierre Lavedan, Paris, 1954, pp.103-108.

Dupont, Marcel, L'Arc de l'Étoile et le Soldat inconnu, Paris, 1958.

Fontaine, Pierre-François-Léonard, Journal 1799-1853, 2 vols., Paris, 1987.

Gaehtgens, Thomas W., "Napoleons Arc de Triomphe," Abandlungen der Akademie des Wissenschaften in Güttingen, 3rd series, vol. XC, 1974.

Rivollet, Georges, L'Arc de triomphe et les oubliés de la Gloire, Paris, 1969.

Rouge, Isabelle, "L'Arc de triomphe de l'Étoile, Panthéon de la France guerrière depuis 1789," to appear.

Saint-Simon, Fernand de, La Place de l'Étoile. Place Charles-de-Gaulle, Paris, 1988.

La Sculpture française du XIXe siècle, exh. cat., Grand Palais, Paris, 10 April-28 July 1986.

Thierry, Jules-Denis, L'Arc de triomphe de l'Étoile, 2nd ed., Paris, 1845.

Captions

Cover

1st: The Arc de Triomphe at the Étoile seen from the Carrousel Arch.
2nd exterior overleaf: one of the two spiral staircases situated in the piers.
4th: photograph taken on 11 November 1998.

BNF: Paris, Bibliothèque nationale de France.

MP, AP: Paris, Médiathèque du patrimoine, Archives photographiques.

Chronology

From left to right, and from top to bottom:

• Political life: Napoleon I, medal, 1804, Paris, Hôtel des Monnaies, MP, AP/CNMHS; Charles X and Louis XVIII, medal, 1829, id.; Louis-Philippe et Marie-Amélie, medal, 1848, id.; Napoléon III, 1855; Third Republic, 1878; "The Sower" by Roty, I.F., 1920; perforation of the Phrygien bonnet by Lindauer, 25 cent. 1933; République by Lagriffoul, 20 cent., 1977; Spirit of the Bastille, engraving atelier of La Monnaie, I.F., 1988 (6 items, coll. Malécot; reprod. Cadet/CNMHS).

• Construction of the Arch: the Champs-Élysées in 1789, engraving, BNF, MP, AP/CNMHS; Chalgrin and Huyot projects, engravings, Berthe/CNMHS; bird's eye view of the Champs-Élysées, engraving, BNF, MP, AP/CNMHS; the Étoile roundabout, engraving, id.; panorama, postcard, coll. Malécot; Arch section, engraving, Berthe/CNMHS.

• Sculpture: Wimille column, Acloque/CNMHS; Carrousel Arch, Lemaître/CNMHS; Spirit of the Bastille, Acloque/CNMHS; Liberty, replica, 1900, Paris, Luxembourg Garden, Acloque/CNMHS.

• Events: model for the marriage of Napoleon, Cadet/CNMHS; Return of Napoleon's Ashes, engraving, BNF, MP, AP/CNMHS; Arrival of the Shah of Persia to Paris, engraving, id.; Paris, 11 November 1920, Gambetta's Tank under the Arch of Triumph, CNMHS; Liberation of Paris, commemorative coin, 1995, coll. Malécot, Cadet/CNMHS; Soccer World Cup, Lemaître/CNMHS.

• Arches of the World: arc du Carrousel, Lemaître/CNMHS; Marble Arch, postcard, 1908, coll. Malécot; Lisbonne Arch, postcard, 1950, coll. Malécot; Arche de la Défense, Revault/CNMHS.

Photographic credits

Source of line drawings: Thierry, 1845.

Altitude, Yann Arthus-Bertrand: 4-5;
BDIC: 24;
BNF: 1b, 18h;
CNMHS, B. Acloque: 34, 36, 40-41, 43, 45, 49b, 62;
P.Berthé: 6, 11h, 13, 27, 35, 37-39, 44-45, 48-49, 53, 55, 59;
P. Cadet: 23b, 25h, 58, 63;
A. Charles: 1st on cover;
P. Lemaître: 29, 33, 42, 50-51, 56-57, 62-64, 2nd on exterior overleaf, 4th on cover;
A. Lonchampt: 25b, 46-47;
É. Revault: 26, 52, 54;
French documentation.
A. Guyomard, interior cover page;
Giraudon: 3g;
Harlingue-Violiet: 21b;
R. Liot: 7h, 14;
MP, AP/CHMHS: 7b, 11b, 18b, 19, 21h, 28(3);
Photothèque des Musées de la Ville de Paris: 17b;
Tournazet: 1h;
RMN: 8-9, 12, 15, G. Blot: 28(2), 28(4), Jean: 17h, 28(2), H. Lewandowski: 28(1);
Roger-Violiet:60-61;
Violiet: 23h.

Coordinating editor
Vincent Bouvet

Coordination of documents
Claude Malécot

Translator
Barbara Shapiro Comte

Copy editor
Elizabeth Ayre

Production coordinator
Carine Merse

Design
Atalante/Paris

Production
Claude Gentiletti/Paris

Graphics
Pol Eger/Paris

Photoengraving
Scann'Ouest/
La Chapelle-sur-Erdre

Printing
Phénix impression/
Bagneux

Dépôt légal:
April 2000